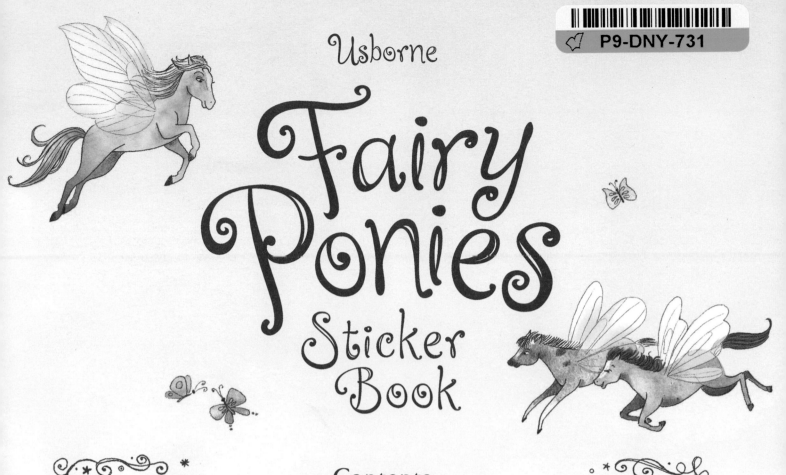

Usborne Fairy Ponies Sticker Book

Contents

Illustrated by Barbara Bongini

Designed by Brenda Cole

Written by Lesley Sims and Zanna Davidson

Holly and the Fairy Ponies

Meet Holly and her friends. Holly has discovered a magical world...
Hidden inside the old oak tree, at the end of her
great-aunt's garden, she found wonderful
Pony Island where fairy ponies live.

Holly

To enter Pony Island, Holly
sprinkles herself with magic dust.
Glittering sparkles surround her
and she shrinks to the size of a fairy.

Puck

Holly's best friend on
Pony Island. He's a brave
little pony and always
eager for an adventure.

Dandelion

Puck's friend. Another
young fairy pony, friendly
and mischievous, she likes
playing tricks on Puck.

Pony Queen

The noble, powerful
ruler of Pony Island.
Butterflies flutter
around her wherever
she goes.

Bluebell

Puck's mother and
one of Pony Island's Spell
Keepers, the most magical and
important ponies on the island. She has a
gleaming coat and a long flowing mane.

Princess Rosabel

The Pony Queen's niece. She lives on nearby Waterfall Island, across the Rainbow Sea.

Dancer

Puck's uncle and another Spell Keeper, dedicated to protecting Pony Island. He's ready to fly to the rescue at a moment's notice.

Spray

A river pony who lives in the Singing River. His body is pearly green and his eyes are ocean blue.

Izagard

A wise old wizard pony, who lives in a cottage in the High Mountains. He has a silvery coat and an icy white mane.

Willow

One of the unicorns who lives on Pony Island in the Enchanted Woods.

Shadow

An evil pony who has turned against the Pony Queen and wants to rule Pony Island himself.

Pony Island

Find the sticker of Puck giving Holly a ride above the island, and add fairy ponies, trees and butterflies to the scene.

Unicorn Prince's Palace

Home of the Unicorn Prince, ruler of the unicorns who live on Pony Island. The palace's golden gates are hidden from strangers behind enchanted vines.

Magic Pony Pools

Sparkling pools with amazing healing powers. Visited by the Pony Queen every day for her Royal Bath Time.

Dark Forest

Lake of Gilded Lilies

Dancing Waterfall

Unicorn Prince's Palace

Enchanted Woods

Pony Magic School

Magic Pony Pools

Woody Glade

Sunlit Sea

High Mountains

Izagard's House

Everlasting Rainbow

Izagard's House

A snug cottage in the High Mountains, filled with books of magic and folklore.

Summer Palace

Rainbow Mountain

Forever Flower Meadow

Rainbow Shore

Summer Palace

The elegant home of the Pony Queen. Built of gleaming white marble, it houses the Necklace of Wishes which can grant the wearer's deepest desire.

Butterfly Valley

Silver Stream

Singing River

Singing River

Home of the river ponies, who are summoned by whistling a special tune.

Meadows

Entrance from the Great Oak

N
W   E
S

Welcome Holly!

Holly is being welcomed to Pony Island. Flying ponies come to join in the fun, scattering flowers as they go. Birds swoop from the trees and butterflies flit around on rainbow wings.

The Singing River

Holly and Puck are swimming through the warm waters of the Singing River. Shimmering fish and curious sea creatures dart and dive around them.

Summer Palace Picnic

On the lawns of the Summer Palace, the Pony Queen is having
a garden party. Excited ponies gather, bringing baskets laden
with treats. Soon the table is filled with juicy berries,
luscious cakes and sparkling honeydew juice.

High above Pony Island

Holly clings to Puck's back as he soars over the Summer Palace.
All of Pony Island is spread out below them, and flying ponies
fill the sky, gliding through the glorious blue.

The Dressing-up Contest

It's the day of the grand dressing-up contest. Everyone puts on elaborate headdresses and elegant garlands. Some fairy ponies decorate their tails too. As the excitement mounts, who will the Pony Queen choose as this year's winner?

Izagard's House

Deep in the misty mountains sits Izagard's snug cottage. Woodland creatures chatter and play, while robins peck at the snow, and squirrels chase each other in the trees.

Unicorn Palace

In the gardens of the Unicorn Prince, Holly
and Puck are playing tag around the
fountain. Unicorns wander the lawns,
or fly overhead with the birds.

Playing on Rainbow Shore

It's a beautiful sunny day and everyone has come to the beach.
Holly, Puck and the other fairy ponies splash in the waves.
Dolphins leap for joy, while seagulls strut along the sand.

Pony Band Party

As dusk falls and the stars begin to twinkle, the
Pony Band strikes up. Lively melodies fill the air.
Holly and the fairy ponies dance until they're
breathless — and even the Pony Queen joins in.

The Lake of Gilded Lilies

Holly, Puck and Rosabel are floating across the Lake
of Gilded Lilies, carried by friendly turtles. Fish dart
around the lily pads and a frog hops up to say hello.

Digital manipulation by Nick Wakeford

Based on the **Young Reading Fairy Ponies** series, part of the **Usborne Reading Programme**.
First published in 2016 by Usborne Publishing Ltd, Usborne House, 83-85 Saffron Hill, London EC1N 8RT, England.
www.usborne.com Copyright © 2016 Usborne Publishing Ltd. The name Usborne and the devices ⊕ ♀ are Trade Marks of Usborne

Pages 2-3

Pages 4-5

Pages 6-7

Pages
12-13

Pages 14-15

Pages 16-17

Pages 18-19

Page 24